Around the World

An Illustrated ABC Book
from the students of
Columbus College of Art and Design

Columbus College of Art & Design
60 Cleveland Avenue, Columbus, OH 43215

Around the World: An Illustrated ABC Book
ISBN: 978-1503344518

Logo illustration by Amber Phillips.
Edited by Adam Osgood and Rebecca Zomchek.

The illustrations in this book were created by the
students of *Illustration for Graphic Design,* taught
by Rebecca Zomchek and Adam Osgood.

To think. To do. To reflect.
To unleash your power to shape culture and commerce.

Columbus College of Art & Design
60 Cleveland Avenue, Columbus, OH 43215

www.ccad.edu

"Typography is the perfect combination of math, science, and design to create one of the most unappreciated forms of art. The ability of tiny, computer rendered characters to come together and create an emotional response is like black magic. Of the thousands of typefaces out there, most of which are fairly similar to one another, each one can be used in an infinite amount of ways to create any desired effect. Even the same typeface can be used to broadcast entirely different messages based on any small context changes made by the designer. Graphic design is an ever-evolving medium that won't slow down any time soon."

-Joseph Van Hove,
Advertising/Graphic Design Major at CCAD

"Each letter of the alphabet is a steadfast loyal soldier in a great army of words, sentences, paragraphs, and stories. One letter falls, and the entire language falters."

—Vera Nazarian, *The Perpetual Calendar of Inspiration*

this book is a collection of Drop Cap examples from the Columbus College of Art and Design's "Illustration for Graphic Design" Class of 2014. The class is designed to introduce graphic design students the power of visual storytelling and expose them to the process of picture making from a different artistic perspective. Hand lettering is a fantastic example of the beautiful harmony that can work between more traditional art skills and graphic design.

Around the World challenged our students to illustrate drop cap* designs based on the first letter in the name of a city from anywhere in the world. The designers researched their chosen city, collecting written and visual data about their chosen city including details about the history, food, fashion, art, and architecture of that location. Using this research the students created illustrations to highlight their cities' diversity and distinctive qualities, capturing glimpses of unique cultural influence from around the globe.

This is Columbus College of Art and Design's second printed collection of the Drop Cap project and the students have put together an excellent compendium of work showcasing multiple styles and artistic problem solving. We hope to continue this tradition and level of design work for years to come.

—Rebecca Zomchek & Adam Osgood
Assistant Professors, Illustration Department, CCAD

*Drop Cap: In book publishing the first letter of a paragraph that is enlarged to "drop" down two or more lines, as in the next paragraph. Drop caps are often seen at the beginning of novels, where the top of the first letter of the first word lines up with the top of the first sentence and drops down to the four or fifth sentence to the beginning of a section (webopedia.com). Or: A large, often highly decorated letter set at the beginning of a chapter, verse, or paragraph (thefreedictionary.com).

Aberdeen, Scotland
Celtic knots frame Scottish claymores, referencing
the city's ancient cultural heritage.

Shane Cornell

Albuquerque, New Mexico.
Here you'll find a vast desert that hosts the
International Balloon Fiesta, as well as the setting
of the television series *Breaking Bad.*

Nadia Ouenniche

Babylon (Iraq)
The winged lion, in the style of classical relief sculptures, suggests
the city's iconic architecture and alludes to biblical symbolism.

Shane Cornell

Barcelona, Spain
The aerial view of Barcelona shows
the cubic design of the city.

Faye Holmes

Cambridge, England
Cambridge is known for prestigious colleges
and historic architecture.

Zachary Perry

Chiba, Japan
Futa, the famous standing red panda, lives
in Chiba City Zoological Park.

Ashleigh Harvey

Detroit, Michigan
The "Motor City" is a symbol for the
American automobile industry.

Tim Couger

Dublin, Ireland
The harp-shaped Samuel Beckett Bridge was designed
by Santiago Calatrava and opened in 2009.

Zachary Perry

Edinburgh, Scotland
Presiding over the city's skyline, Edinburgh Castle is a
historic fortress that sits on Castle Rock.

Ashleigh Harvey

Erevan, Armenia
Diamonds are a key export for Armenia, while pomegranates
symbolize fertility and good fortune.

Amber Phillips

Florence, Italy
The old-style typeface and floral pattern celebrate
Florence as the birthplace of the Renaissance.

Ashleigh Harvey

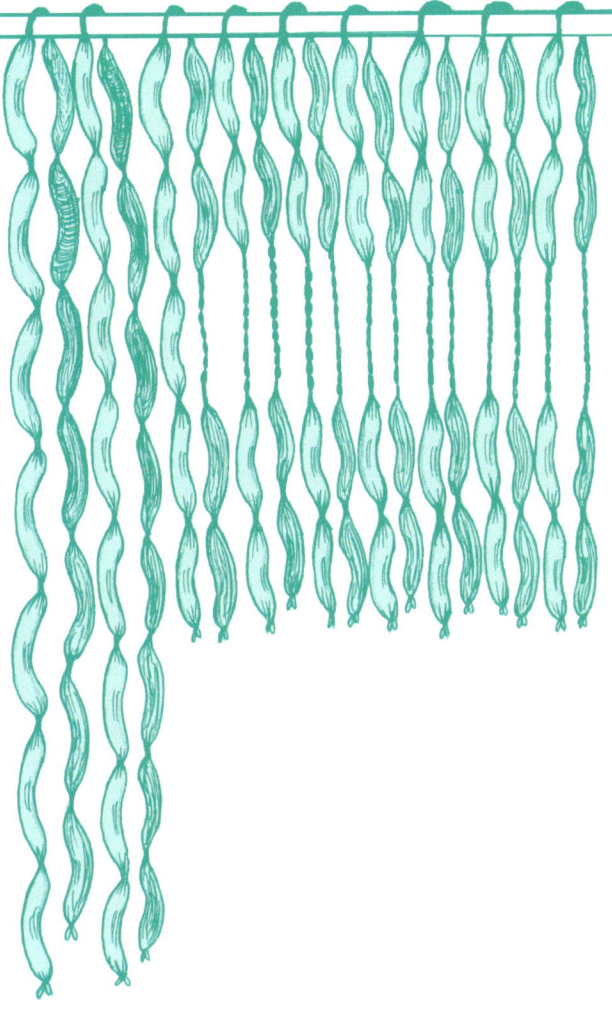

Frankfurt, Germany
Whenever you think of Frankfurt,
you just think of sausage.

Faye Holmes

Giza, Egypt
Famous for some of the most impressive ancient monuments
in the world, including the Great Pyramid of Giza.

Joseph Van Hove

Glasgow, Scotland
Known for rolling hills and beautiful architecture.

Kaitlyn Tugend

Helsinki, Finland
Inspired by a classic Marimekko pattern, the letterform celebrates
the functionalist approach to design that Finland is famous for.

Amber Phillips

Hong Kong, China
Hong Kong has a lot of interesting street
foods for people to enjoy.

Faye Holmes

Ísafjörður, Iceland
Known for its valleys and rivers as well as its Celtic roots.

Hannah Schumick

Istanbul, Turkey
Istanbul is famous for its wide array of bazaars and marketplaces;
stocked with ceramics, Turkish rugs, evil eyes, and spices.

Rachel Kalaycio

Jaén, Spain
The Jaén Cathedral is a Renaissance-style
cathedral built from 1570 through 1802.

Skylar Bridges

Jaén, Spain
The olive oil capital of the world.

Lane Keiser Beachler

Kaalawai, Hawaii
Coral reef imagery celebrates the ocean and
marine life of this coastal city.

Callie Whiteman

Kiev, Ukraine
The Dnieper River flows through Kiev towards the Black Sea.

Andreas Kallinicou

Las Vegas, Nevada
A destination for gambling, known for their famous welcome
sign and replicas of monuments from across the world.

Kevin Butler

London, England
London is known for many things, including: Big Ben, tea, the
Queen's Guard, rainy weather, and the first traffic light.

Zoe Rodriguez

Milan, Italy
The Duomo di Milano, constructed over a period of 500
years from 1386 to 1965, is the most famous landmark
in Milan, sporting an array of architectural styles.

Ai Negishi

Moscow, Russia
St. Basil's Cathedral is recognized for its distinctive
architecture, bright colors, and decorative patterns.

Scott Warfel

Nantucket, Massachusetts
Historically known as a whaling port, the island town
inspired Herman Melville's *Moby Dick*.

Callie Whiteman

New Delhi, India
New Delhi has the second largest
abundance of birds in the world.

Tyler Shaffer

Odessa, Ukraine
This floral pattern is inspired by the by the crisp lines
and shapes in classic Ukrainian embroidery.

Ai Negishi

Osaka, Japan
The Sangatsubasho is a professional Sumo tournament
held annually at Osaka Prefectural Gymnasium.

Matthew Dixon

Paris, France
Bread is essential to French cuisine.

Tyler Shaffer

Patras, Greece
Greece's "Gate to the West" is an important port of trade
and communication with Italy and Western Europe.

Ai Negishi

Quartz Hill, California
Each year, Quartz Hill celebrates the Almond Blossom Festival.

Hayley Farris

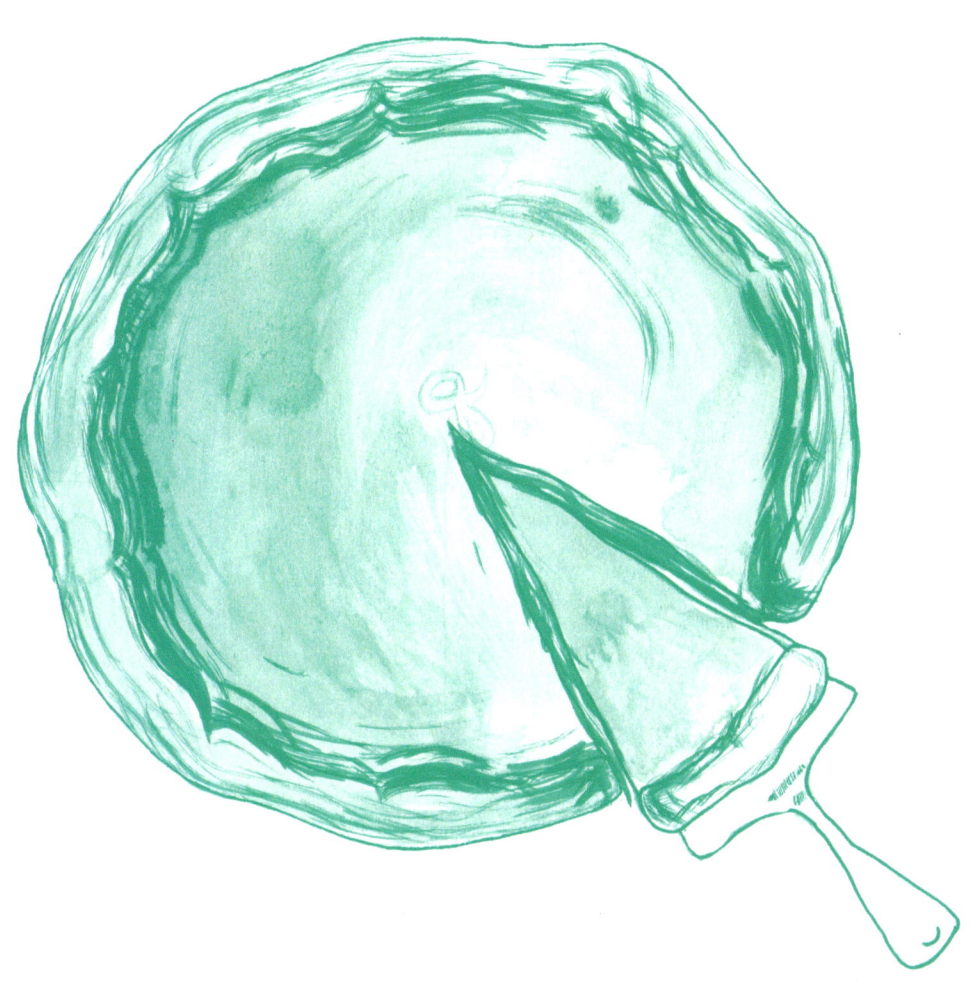

Quebec City, Quebec
Tourtière is a meat pie that residents of Quebec
enjoy eating in the winter season.

Faye Holmes

Reno, Nevada
"The Biggest Little City in the World,"
Reno is famous for its casinos.

Alecx Stasko

Rio de Janeiro, Brazil
Ornate designs and texture are popular on
costumes worn during "Carnival".

Angelique Williams

San Salvador, El Salvador
San Salvador is known for its varied landscape including
mountains, hills, rivers, lakes, and the Boquerón Volcano.

Jeannie Leary

Stockholm, Sweden
Stockholm is known for many things including castles, Viking heritage, the longest days and nights, and meatballs.

Zoe Rodriguez

Tokyo, Japan
Tokyo is known as an urban area that hasn't
forgotten its Ancient Japanese roots.

Rachel Kalaycio

Tokyo, Japan
Godzilla sparked a great film culture for Tokyo and influenced
modern-day monster films, such as *Cloverfield* and *Pacific Rim*.

Caleb Wolff

Ubatuba, Brazil
The surf is always alive in Ubatuba.

Skylar Bridges

Urgon, Afghanistan
Once a provincial capitol and the site
of many influential sieges.

Mary Elizabeth Carlin

Vatican City
Different individuals interpret religious text in different
ways, much like the results of a Rorschach test.

TJ Boster

Venice, California
This lively beach front area of Los Angeles is known
for its ocean walk, populated with body builders,
surfers, hippies, and unique street performers.

Mary Elizabeth Carlin

Washington, D.C.
Also known as District of Columbia, Washington, D.C.
is a unique federal district created specifically to be
the seat of government in the United States.

Scott Warfel

Wellington, New Zealand
The wellington cable car tracks connect the city's main shopping
street and a popular suburb which overlooks the central city.

Tyler Shaffer

Xenia, Ohio
Holding the record for second largest tornado in history,
the Shawnee Indians called it "the place of the devil winds."

Mary Elizabeth Carlin

Xi'an, China
The Terracotta Army is a collection of thousands of sculptures
representing the armies of Qin Shi Huang, the first Emperor of China.

Matthew Dixon

York, England
Emblematic lions and intersecting stripes are inspired
by patterns found in the city's flag.

Shane Cornell

York, England
One of York's major attractions is the York Minster,
one of the largest cathedrals in Northern Europe.

Kevin Butler

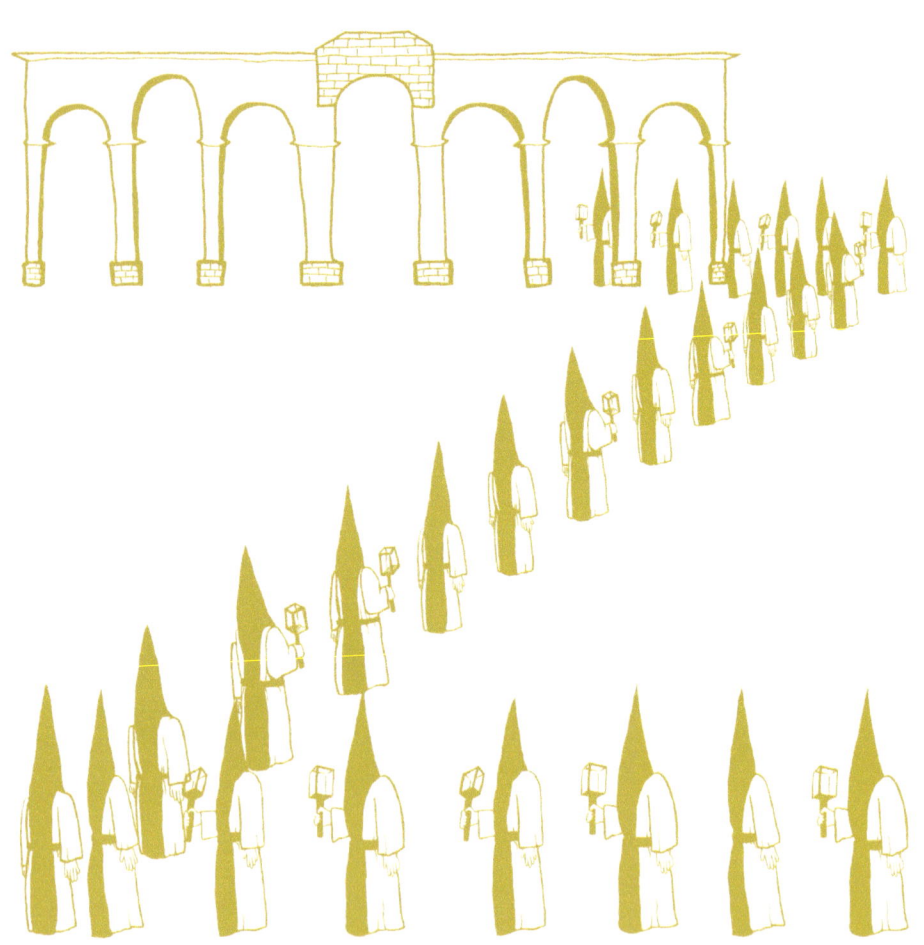

Zamora, Spain
Holy Week is celebrated by 16 Catholic religious brotherhoods and fraternities that perform penance processions on the streets of the city.

Jeannie Leary

Zürich
The Limmat River flows through Old Town, a historic
district known for its Medieval architecture.

Zachary Perry

Lane Keiser Beachler: Jaén
lanebeachler@gmail.com, behance.net/LaneBeachler
The best part about being a designer is getting to create things every day, especially because it's something I love to do. People I care about inspire me to do my best work. I know they expect a lot from me and it feels really good to come out with more than they even thought I would.

TJ Boster: Vatican City
tj.boster@gmail.com, behance.net/TBoster
I come from a Graffiti background so the things I love about typography are the way individuals can take words and letters and communicate numerous messages while distorting the classical form of a letter. Typographical Anarchy!!!!

Skylar Bridges: Jaén, Ubatuba
skyebridges25@yahoo.com, behance.net/SkylarBridges
Designing or illustrating the style and character of type is my favorite thing about Typography. Creating my own typography gives me the chance to express certain feelings that a standard typeface couldn't, telling a story thought the fluidity of the line work.

Kevin Butler: Las Vegas, York
KButler.2@go.ccad.edu, behance.net/KevinButler
The best part about being a designer is that there are no limits to what you can create. Nothing is cut and dry, and you can always put your own spin on things. My favorite thing about typography is that is can be very simple yet beautiful. It doesn't have to be over the top to be something special.

Mary Elizabeth Carlin: Urgon, Venice, Xenia
mcarlin.1@go.ccad.edu, behance.net/MaryCarlin
My favorite thing about typography is the importance it plays in our daily lives and the freedom of information it communicates. I love the ability typography has to transcend the realm of simple words on a page; the feeling, aesthetics, and sensory aspects the printed letters themselves can implement in a design or message.

Shane Cornell: Aberdeen, Babylon, York
scknight1994@gmail.com, behance.net/Shane_Cornell
My favorite thing about typography is how human it is. It opens up millions of ways to give simple letters and words an individual voice as unique as the person creating it. My unfaltering love for all things medieval, and antique inspires me to look to history for inspiration. I particularly enjoy the beautiful colors & lines of stained glass as well as the complex intricate details of Celtic knots.

Tim Couger: Detroit
TCouger.1@go.ccad.edu, behance.net/tim1
The best part of being a designer is working through the creative process, and seeing something start out as a small thought and made into something polished and finalized. In order to have a successful design your work should meet a set of goals that will better communicate to an audience. Making these goals is how I start a design, but meeting them is what motivates me.

Matt Dixon: Osaka, Xi'an
dixondesign@icloud.com, mdixondesign.com
The expressiveness in typography is what makes it great. For a crude example, which looks more exciting and expressive to look at "loud" or "LOUD"? One can be read and forgotten quickly, but the other can create an emotion and stick with you for a least a little bit.

Hayley Farris: Quartz Hill
HFarris.1@go.ccad.edu, behance.net/hayleyfarris
My favorite thing about typography is its ability to effect whatever it is being used for. Handwritten typography is my favorite, and I hope to pursue a career where I can use this skill. Seeing how art has helped me grow to become the person I am is what inspires me the most, as well as the success of the people I look up to, and the success of my peers.

Ashleigh Harvey: Chiba, Edinburgh, Florence
ashleighmharvey@hotmail.com
My favorite thing about typography is how interesting it can really make something. You would just think that type is boring, but it can be so interesting especially when it's handwritten. It makes it more personal and no other font is just like it.

Rachel Kalaycio: Istanbul, Tokyo
rkalaycio@yahoo.com, behance.net/rkalaycio
The best part about being a designer is the satisfaction of finishing a project. I really enjoy seeing my work being used in books, on t-shirts, and more. It's exciting to know that my work could go anywhere. My favorite thing about typography is the fact that there are so many ways to illustrate the letters of words to tell a visual story, convey a message, or make a statement.

Jeannie Leary: San Salvador, Zamora
JLeary.1@go.ccad.edu, Jeannieleary.tumblr.com
The best part about being a designer is the ability to impact people. Whether it's with words, color choice, shape, or line, designers have a message we want to communicate. Designers can make you question something you've never even thought about and I think that's pretty cool.

Ai Negishi: Milan, Odessa, Pero
ai.g.negishi@gmail.com, behance.net/anegishi
The best thing about being a designer is that I have an opportunity to design things that are seen by people everyday. My favorite thing about typography is that fonts can express mood or emotions without a picture. It's always fun to experiment with the size and color. I am inspired by simple and clean designs that are soothing to my eyes. I'm usually attracted to ambitious compositions using the grid system.

Nadia Ouenniche: Albuquerque
nouenniche.1@go.ccad.edu, behance.net/NadiaOuenniche
My favorite thing about typography is that it can create a whole new identity to a word. Whether it is minor or major changes to the type, a word can emit a completely different emotion. What inspires me to do my best work is that I don't have to change who I am. Just completing a piece makes me feel a sense of accomplishment and that I am a step closer to completing my goals.

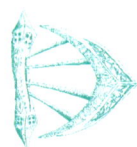

Zachary Perry: Dublin, Cambridge, Zurich
zmperry1@gmail.com, behance.net/ZacharyPerry
My favorite thing about typography is appreciating the fact that it can be a beautiful art form. When given the respect it deserves, what can be provoked with type is limitless. I believe that may be what I love most about it. My future inspires me to do my best work. I want to be able to provide for my family, while enjoying my career in doing so.

Amber Phillips: Erevan, Helsinki
aphillips.3@go.ccad.edu, amber-arts.tumblr.com
My favorite thing about typography is the ability to make words come alive and deliver their message as a whole as well as each individual letter itself. What inspires me to do my best work is my love for good illustration and design; to get better and become the best person and artist I can be.

Zoe Rodriguez: London, Stockholm
zoerodriiguez@gmail.com, behance.net/zoerodrgz
Typography has always been one of my biggest passions. More than just being a simple font, typography for me is more like illustrating with words. I love hand lettering and get to draw my own words. What inspires me the most is my mom, being the daughter of such a talented human being makes me want to be better every day.

Hannah Schumick: Ísafjörður
HSchumick.1@go.ccad.edu, behance.net/HannahSchumick
Typography is the backbone of graphic design. Without strong type, it's almost impossible to convey an idea to an audience. Typography is an art form all on its own, it can be super simple or extremely detailed. Typography is the graphic designers bread and butter, and that's why I like it so much, it hammers my ideas home and really makes a piece.

Tyler Shaffer: New Delhi, Paris, Wellington
tshaffer.1@go.ccad.edu, behance.net/tshaffer_1
I think the best part about being a designer is having the freedom to experiment and change. There is never just one predictable obstacle or solution for each task or project. As a designer, not only can I convey an idea through the actual word itself, but through various uses of imagery as well.

Alecx Stasko: Reno
Astasko.1@go.ccad.edu, behance.net/Astasko
My favorite thing about typography is how versatile it is. I'm enthralled that specific type faces can evoke certain emotions and bring you back into a nostalgic memory or place. My best work comes from topics that I am passionate about. I love creating impactful and controversial pieces of art that can help create emotion from the viewer.

Kaitlyn Tugend: Glasgow
tugend.k@gmail.com, behance.net/febish
Since I am able to visually and creatively solve problems I rarely find myself bored creatively which I believe helps me learn and grow constantly as a person and as a designer. Every single day I do something I never thought I could do, something that I thought was impossible. Constantly being challenged to become the best I can be and seeing the end result of something I put all of my effort into is my greatest motivation.

Joseph Van Hove: Giza
jvanhove.1@go.ccad.edu, behance.net/joevanhove
What inspires me the most about design is the vast amount of material that has been created in graphic design's short existence. Graphic designers draw in so much from their surroundings, thus in the past century the world has witnessed an explosion of design that is rich in culture and is greatly diverse in different regions of the world. With so much to take in and learn from, one could spend more than their lifetime immersed in graphic design.

Scott Warfel: Moscow, Washington DC
SWarfel.1@go.ccad.edu, scottbyron.format.com
What inspires me to do my best work is when I travel to different cities. Each city I've been to has left an impact on who I stand for, and where I want to go. I want to leave that similar impact on others with my designs I can leave behind in each city I visit. There are a lot of people to connect with in the world and only a limited amount of time.

Callie Whiteman: Kaalawai, Nantucket
CWhiteman.1@go.ccad.edu, behance.com/calliewhiteman
I get to make the world a better place!
As Paula Scher said, "Words have meaning, type has spirit, and the combination is spectacular."

Angelique Williams: Rio de Janeiro
Awilliams.3@go.ccad.edu, behance.net/angelw
My favorite thing about typography is the array of different styles and sizes that are available for use and how easy it is making my own typography for my designs. What inspires me to do my best work is my thought of "what if this is found 10 years from now would I be proud of it?" If not then I would have wished I did better back then, and I never want that situation to happen.

Caleb Wolff: Tokyo
CWolff.2@go.ccad.edu, behance.net/calebwolff
Having the ability to visually communicate with an audience you are trying to reach, even if you are not a part of that audience, is a very precise talent which few are born with. A word communicates a message. Play around with how that word is written and portrayed and you give the message a deeper or even a different meaning. Which can make a word hold 1000 words.

www.ingramcontent.com/pod-product-compliance
Lightning Source LLC
Chambersburg PA
CBHW040323010626
45792CB00024B/2101